CREATING THE IDEAL ADOPTION PROFILE

CREATING THE IDEAL ADOPTION PROFILE

RUSSELL ELKINS

Creating the Ideal Adoption Profile
How to Get Noticed by Potential Birthparents, Writing the Perfect "Dear Birthmother" Letter, Choosing the Right Profile Pictures, and More…
part 2 of the series: 30 Minute Guides to Headache-Free Open Adoption Parenting
By Russell Elkins
©2019 Russell Elkins

series line editors: Kim Foster, Jenna Lovell
series content editors: Martin Casey, Cathy Watson Childs

Cover photo and author photo by Jammie Elkins Photography
Cover design by Inky's Nest Design
Interior book layout by Inky's Nest Design

ISBN: 978-1-950741-06-9

Inky's Nest Publishing

RussellElkins.com
2nd edition
First edition printed in 2013 in the United States of America

CONTENTS

Introduction

Adoption is one of the most beautiful things a family could ever experience. My family has been blessed twice through this miracle.

In the past, adoption agencies and caseworkers took on the responsibility of deciding the best placement for a child. Many agencies went with a "first come, first served" approach, which meant that adoptive couples had to get in line and wait, and the amount of time they needed to wait depended upon how many people were ahead of them in line.

That is not true anymore. In the vast majority of cases now, the biological parents of a child who is going to be placed for adoption make the decision on the best placement. After potential birthparents have chosen an adoption agency, one of their next steps is to browse the agency's list of people who have already been approved and are waiting to adopt. Some agencies have them do this by looking through a physical scrapbook of hopeful adoptive parents, but most agencies have these profiles available online. Being able to choose which home they feel is right for their child can bring some comfort to their stressful situation.

These changes have made it increasingly important for hopeful adoptive parents to create an ideal adoption profile. An ideal profile can help catch the eye of potential birthparents by more effectively showing how their homes work, look and feel. Because few (if any) adoption agencies use the "first come, first served" method anymore, some couples are chosen very quickly while others, who might not have the right tools, wait for many years.

My wife and I spent a lot of time preparing own family's adoption profiles, and I spent even more time putting this book together. I have seen a lot of profiles and noticed a lot of mistakes. Some of them force me to say, "That profile is enough to turn any potential birthparent away. Nobody is ever going to choose that couple." I have heard countless people say they know God will make the adoption happen in His time. I have also heard some birthparents say that when the time came for them to choose, that their decision was made clear through divine inspiration. By no means do I discount divine inspiration or the hand of God in our lives, but at the same time God tends to help those who put forth the effort to help themselves.

There is never any guarantee that hopeful adoptive couples will be chosen quickly, or even at all, but there are things that can be done to greatly increase the odds in your favor.

Not all adoption agencies list hopeful adoptive parents in the same way. Different agencies will have various rules and methods for creating your profile. Some use scrapbooks, others do everything online. Still others will use a combination of those two as well as other resources. Some agencies want one profile letter per couple, some want two (one from each of the hopeful adoptive parents). Some ask for the letter to be written in first person, while others prefer third person, and some prefer a combination of the two (like my own family profile letter). Confusing? Yes. Here is the point: The basic principles will be the same on how to make your profile stand out, no matter the agency's regulations and format.

1

CHOOSING THE RIGHT PROFILE PICTURE

I know it sounds cliché for me to say, but you never get a second chance to make a first impression, and a picture is worth a thousand words. Clichés are cliché because they are true.

Whether it is a small thumbnail-sized photo or a large high quality image, the first thing any potential birthparent will see is your profile picture. This is true regardless of which website or agency you use. Because of this, the profile picture is *extremely* important. If your profile picture does not capture their interest within one or two seconds, it will not matter how awesome the rest of your profile is because they will skim right past you to the next profile.

That would be a problem, so how do we solve it?

Does Your Profile Picture Stand Out?

Imagine a thousand beautiful long-stemmed red roses all bunched together in an enormous bouquet. Now imagine that somewhere randomly placed in that beautiful bouquet is a single white rose. This illustration is perhaps the most important concept in choosing a profile picture. While many people might protest and say they think red roses are the most beautiful flower, when that red rose is bunched up with all the other red roses, it simply blends in with the rest. It is difficult to notice any individual red rose, even if it is the most beautiful one out of all of the red roses. The white rose, though, will practically jump out of the vase even if it is not as beautiful as the red ones. Aesthetic appeal is important in your profile picture, but it is much more important to stand out.

Your number one goal for your cover profile picture is to make someone stop long enough to notice you. *Nobody is going to choose you because of this one picture.* That is not the goal of this photo. This picture is meant to grab someone's attention. This picture is simply an invitation to click on your profile—an invitation to come in and get to know you a little better.

So what does that mean for you? It means simply that you do not do what everyone else is doing.

The majority of couples without children tend to choose a picture that would work well for a wedding announcement. And couples who already have children tend to choose a family portrait that would look beautiful on their living room wall. Do not do this. While you may look beautiful in your engagement-style photo, the problem is that you will be just another red rose.

Take a moment to browse the other profile pictures where yours will be displayed. Note what everyone else is doing and be intentionally different. The longer the list of couples hoping to adopt, the more unique you may need to be.

If you consider yourself creative, you can come up with something on your own to make your picture stand out. If you are not, there is nothing wrong with borrowing someone else's idea. It would be a bad idea for you to copy the idea of a profile within your same adoption agency, but you can always go to the website of a different agency or peruse profiles somewhere like adoption.com for ideas.

What Does Your Profile Picture *Say*?

Going back to our cliché phrase from before, a picture is worth a thousand words. Well, if you were to put your picture into words, what would it say? And what would you want it to say? This is essential no matter how many other couples are listed around you.

Let's start to answer this question by first asking another one: What qualities do you think a birthmother (or birthfather) cares about? Go ahead, grab a notebook right now and make a list of what you think they care about and you will have a list of things you want your picture to say.

I spent a lot of time asking birthparents what they had looked for when they were choosing someone to adopt their child, and guess what! Not a single one of them mentioned anything about whether adoptive couples had pretty hair or whether they were dressed nicely. Still, that tends to be what most hopeful adoptive parents focus on when producing their own picture. Don't get me wrong, having an unkempt appearance will turn anybody off before they can even blink, okay? But the birthparents I talked to used descriptive words like: loving, fun, close-knit family, and so on. And those words do not have much to do with hair and clothes.

The typical family picture will cause the onlooker to say, "Yep, they're a handsome family." But it will not usually push someone to go further and say, "I can see how much they love each other." The typical engagement-style couple's photo would not make someone think, "Wow, they look fun."

If your main goal is to look "fun," you will still want it to be a close-up shot of your faces, but use a picture of you doing something fun. Or maybe consider a candid photo taken while you were laughing together so that your smiles are large and genuine.

Another way to make your picture speak to any onlooker is to make it talk about something that makes you unique.

You could bring some of your interests into the picture. I am a musician and my wife is a photographer. These interests make us unique. So, in the profile picture from our first adoption, I can be seen holding my acoustic guitar and my wife is standing next to me with her camera. This made it so we were no longer just two faces, but we were real people who do something interesting. It said something about us.

It will be nearly impossible to nail every adjective you think a potential birthparent might be looking for in one picture. With regards to our first profile picture— the one where I am holding my guitar and my wife has her camera— I would not say it screamed out "loving" or "tightly-knit," but it did say, "interesting, fun, active." You will need to decide which descriptive words are most important to you, and which ones you want your profile photo to say.

Should You Be Afraid of Looking Cheesy?

I can say without hesitation and without embarrassment that both of our profile pictures were cheesy. But "cheesy" and "stupid" are not synonyms. For goodness' sake, it should be obvious you do not want to look stupid!

When we were putting together our first profile picture, we asked a friend what she did for theirs and she said they put a cartoon character border around their picture. That is the cheesiness I am talking about. Sure, they knew a cartoon character border was cheesy, but they also knew that "boring" is much worse than "cheesy." The cartoon character border idea was not for us, but we did put a bright red border around our picture to make it stand out. A red border would not be something we would do for a photo to hang on our wall, but among other profile pictures it screamed, "Hey! Look at me!" and it worked. Especially since our profile was only one among so many, cheesy was better than boring.

Does the Quality matter?

Image quality matters. Nothing says, "This adoption is not very important to me," like someone who does not put forth the effort required to put a quality picture on the front page of their profile. You are about to spend a lot of money on the adoption process, so if you need to invest in a new camera or hire a local photographer, make that an essential part of your budget alongside everything else. If you do not like that idea, chances are one of your friends has a decent camera and they will be willing to help you out. Again, you are not going to get a second chance at your first impression.

Do You Need to Crop the Profile Picture?

For some agencies, cropping does not matter. With others it is extremely important. It depends on the Web sites on which you will be listed.

For many agencies, such as the one my wife and I used, there is a main page of profiles where the hopeful adoptive couples' profile photos are shown as small thumbnail images. This is done so that multiple profiles can be listed on the same page.

Thumbnails are square, not rectangular, but almost every camera takes a rectangular picture. What that means is that your photo will not fit properly into the space provided if you do not crop it to be square. You will either have black space above and below your photo, like watching a movie on an old square television, or, if the photograph was taken vertically that wasted space will show up on the left and right sides. That basically wastes a third of the already tiny space given for your thumbnail image, and that is the same as having a smaller picture. You want all the size and exposure you can get.

What is the point of all this? Well, on the home page of the agency my wife and I used, over fifty percent of the photos were not cropped square. This made those that had been properly cropped seem twice as big. This can be a real advantage on that type of listing.

How Much of Your Bodies Should Be Showing?

For the most part, you want to waste the least amount of space as possible on your profile picture. The decision on how close to stand to the camera or how closely to crop the photograph will depend on what you plan to do. Whether your agency or website lists profiles with large or small photographs, if you are seen to be smaller than the others you are going to stand out less. Unused extra space around you (grass, trees, etc.) means you are farther away, which means you are smaller, which is bad.

On the other hand, if colors or something in the background are great for catching attention, it may be a good idea to go ahead and let the background pull some of its own weight. It all depends on the situation. Getting in close can be a little tough if you have a large family you are trying to squeeze into the shot.

Does the Background Matter?

Colorful backgrounds are a great idea. Interesting things like waterfalls, while they should not overshadow you as the main focus of the picture, are interesting enough to make someone stop and take a look. While they are great for family pictures and engagement photos, backdrops like fireplaces, lawns and brick walls fall into the *red rose* category. They are beautiful, but they are also very common. Leaves in the fall catch the eye. Cherry blossoms in the spring do as well. Standing in front of a colorful wall of graffiti (the artistic kind, not the gangster kind) is fun.

Contrasting colors are a great idea. Red stands out in nature because very few things in nature are red. Background colors like neon green or orange may be too cheesy for the wall in your home, but they'll do a good job at catching someone's eye while they are browsing through photo after photo of handsome couples.

A Few Other Things to Consider:

A lot of people love pets. If you have a cat, dog, horse, pot-bellied pig— whatever— you may want to consider including it in your profile picture. I have heard quite a few birthmothers say they specifically wanted a family who loved animals. Take into consideration, however, that some animals will scare people away. No matter how sweet your dog actually is, if it looks mean, then that is what they are going to see.

Always choose a current photo for your profile picture. Potential birthparents want to know what you are like now, not when you got married, or even what you looked like before you gained sixty pounds. If you get a chance to meet someone in person after they see your profile only to show up bald and old, they are likely to be turned off by your dishonesty. Your agency will have other places inside your profile where you can put your older pictures if you so choose.

Smile big in your picture. Remember, you are a happy, loving person who is a lot of fun. Hopefully this would be common sense to you, but to a lot of people it is not. Soft smiles do not say "happy," they say "pleasant," which comes up short. Pursed-lip glamour shots, straight faced serious expressions— I have seen it all, and nothing says "trust me" like a bright, happy, genuine smile.

Words are a great idea. Whether you are using a photo editing program to write a few words on the photo, or you are holding a chalkboard that says a few clever words, there is something about written words that can make the eye stop to invest a few extra seconds in the image after the first glance. I noticed myself clicking on pictures just to get a better look at what was written across the bottom. Getting someone to stop on your picture long enough to get a look at you is your goal, even if the words you choose are not incredibly profound.

You may want to consider choosing more than one picture that you like for your profile and then putting them all together to have your friends look through them. Do not ask them to pick their favorite. Ask them which one catches their eye first and which one makes them go back for a second look.

Last but not least, once your profile is up and listed, for heaven's sake go look at it. That is yet another thing that should be common sense, but I have seen online profile pictures listed sideways. I have even seen profiles with no picture at all. I have seen profile pictures where Dad is missing from the cover photo but he is in other photos elsewhere in their profile. I will never understand how some people could possibly miss this step because my wife and I checked our profile constantly to make sure everything was just how we wanted it. Our profile was important to us because our adoptions were important to us, and we did our very best to make sure that showed.

What Pictures Should Be Displayed *Inside* the Photo Album?

Up until this point, I have discussed only the cover profile picture. Most agencies have a section separate from the initial profile picture specifically designated for additional images. While the cover photo is meant to grab their attention, now that someone has noticed you and clicked on your profile the primary goal is no longer to simply attract attention. If people are browsing your photo album section, you have already got their attention. You do not need to worry anymore about cropping your pictures square or putting colorful borders around pictures with these photos. Now your goal is to present who you are.

This is your opportunity to let your pictures say the descriptive words you were not able to squeeze into your front profile picture. For example, our first profile picture did not present us as loving or tightly-knit, so my wife and I made sure to include photos inside our profile that did.

Here are a few things to keep in mind with your photo album:

It is up to you to show the fun and interesting things in your life that make you who you are, so include a picture of yourself scrapbooking if that is what you like to do, or riding horses, or coaching a little league team.

One or two old photos can do a good job of showing your own childhood, but they're not necessary. A single picture from your wedding day can be nice, but remember that potential birthparents are interested in who you are now, not in who you once were. So if your old pictures do not help to tell a story about you, leave them out.

Keep safety in mind. You may have thoroughly enjoyed your skydiving trip, but that may scare some people away. You may love hunting, and there is nothing at all wrong with decking yourself out in your orange vest and camo for a good photo op, but do not post any pictures of your five-year-old holding a 12-guage shotgun.

Be careful to avoid make yourself look too busy to take on a child. This is a very common mistake and something a lot of birthmothers told me scared them away from certain profiles. If you have twenty different pictures of you doing twenty different activities, potential birthparents may be left wondering how you are going to squeeze a child into your huge list of hobbies. The same goes with traveling. While it may be really cool that you have been to Paris, Johannesburg, Buenos Aires, and Timbuktu, you do not want someone to ever think you do not have time in your life to just spend quality time at home. Nobody ever places a child for adoption because they cannot provide the amount of air travel time they think their child deserves.

Just like with your profile picture, do not use low quality pictures. These pictures can be regular snapshot photos. They can even be pictures taken by a cell phone camera if the quality is nice, but they still cannot be blurry or look cheap.

2

WRITING THE PROFILE LETTER

The "Profile Letter" will be named differently depending on your adoption agency. I have heard it called things like The Dear Birthmother Letter, The Dear Birthparent Letter, Adoptive Parent Introduction... the list could go on and on.

Knowing what to write in the profile letter is intimidating and daunting for most people. There are a lot of philosophies out there about how to go about it, which makes things even more difficult. The way my wife and I wrote ours in not necessarily the "correct" way to go about it and those who have different preferences are not necessarily wrong. All I can do is tell you about the things birthparents have conveyed to me and the things I took into account when writing our own letter.

Where Do You Begin?

First of all, do not start out by addressing the reader like this: "To whom it may concern..." That is about as impersonal as you could get.

Some agencies want you to begin by addressing the reader as "Dear birthparents," or "Dear birthmother." If they ask you specifically to start this way, by all means do so. If not, I would suggest you do not use either of those two phrases. Some birthparents have informed me that they did not like being called a birthparent back in the time before the child was born because the very definition of that title infers that their child has both been born and placed for adoption. If you want to address them with a title, consider something like "expecting parent" rather than "birthparent."

My wife and I chose not to use any title at all. We just skipped right to our first sentence and went from there, avoiding the whole part about trying to assign them a label.

Whether beginning with a title or skipping right to your first full sentence, one of the best things you can do is to thank them early in the letter. Potential birthparents do not have to choose to place their child for adoption. And if they do choose to place their child, they do not have to consider you. This concept probably sounds obvious to you, but as soon as expecting parents announce that they are considering placing their child for adoption, people come out of the woodwork to show their interest in raising their child. It is very common for grandparents, aunts and uncles, siblings and family friends to put a lot of pressure on them to keep the child in the family tree or close to home. This can weigh very heavily on those considering to place, so one of the worst things you can do is to come off in your profile letter as one of those people who seem to feel entitled to someone else's baby. Potential birthparents do not owe you anything at all. Thanking them sincerely early on in your letter can help you come across in the proper way as someone grateful for any attention they choose to give you.

It is also a good idea to briefly tell why you are choosing to adopt. The reason behind your decision matters greatly to some potential birthparents. Some want to place only with a couple who are incapable of conceiving biological children. I have heard some express that they preferred to place with someone who had always planned to adopt. The list of reasons is lengthy. Include yours early in the letter.

Also, if you have adopted before, you will definitely want to include that as well.

What Should Be In the Introduction?

After you have begun your letter with a quick note of appreciation, it is time to introduce yourself. It is very important that you keep in mind that you are not writing a resume. Nobody in their right mind, no matter how much they love to read, would ever sit at home cozying up to a nice warm blanket and a stack of resumes to pass the time. Resumes are boring. You also do not want to create lists of things that make you awesome. Lists are as boring as resumes.

You want to tell a story. In fact, when I asked one birthmother why she chose the couple to adopt her daughter, she said it was because she fell in love with the way their profile letter started out with the words "Once upon a time..." and continued to tell their story as if it were a fairy tale. While the fairy tale idea would not fit my own personality, it was a clever idea and did a good job illustrating the point I am making here. Paint a picture in the reader's mind. Make it so the reader can actually visualize what you are saying.

Do *not* say it this way:
We met in college when we were both 22 years old. Joseph was studying architecture and Joann was studying to be an elementary school teacher. We dated for about six months before we got engaged and then got married shortly afterward in San Francisco.

28

Rather, you would be better off to write it something like this:

Joseph sat alone one day in the university library. He was going over a set of blueprints he had to turn in for his drafting class when he looked up to see the most beautiful curly red-haired girl he had ever seen. When Joann sat nearby to do some homework, he knew he just had to introduce himself. Before long, she was telling him about her desire to someday be an elementary school teacher and he was talking about plans to go out together that weekend.

You can see how the first example was like reading a list and the second was like reading a story. Stories are much more interesting to read, and the last thing you want to be is boring.

It does take a little bit more time and space to tell a story, but a well-told story is so much easier on the mind. You do not want your story to drag on. You will need to pick the aspects of your story that you feel are most important or you will run the risk of losing their interest if it is not short.

Make sure not to bother with too many boring details. Your goal is to generate interest about you, not to tell everything about yourself. If they take interest in you, you can bore them with your life story later in your blog, over email or in person.

After the Introduction, Then What?

You want to make sure you have a section that includes some of your life interests, not just your life story. This section will talk about the things that make you unique as individuals as well as a couple.

Also, you are going to revisit yet again the list of descriptive words you created earlier with your profile picture. Use examples of your interests that convey all of your descriptive words, including even the ones you already checked off with your photos.

Although you are going off your list of descriptive words, do not *list* your qualities. It is always better to convey one of your interests and let potential birthparents decide for themselves how they would describe you.

Do not say:
We are a very loving couple.

It would be better to say something like:
Once a month Jim has to travel out of town for work. Whenever he does, he and Mary send each other text messages incessantly and count down the minutes until he can be back home with her.

Specific examples are more interesting than generalities.

Do not just say:
Joseph likes sports.

It is only slightly better, but it still comes up short to say:
Joseph loves softball.

You would be more effective if you said something along the lines of this:
Every spring, Joseph loves playing third base on his company's softball team.

What Are Other Things to Keep In Mind In This Section?

Remember that your goal is to come off as someone potential birthparents can relate to. Be real. That is especially true these days when open adoption means they are possibly looking for someone with whom they can have a long-term open adoption relationship.

Talk about how you love your spouse or significant other. This can be important because oftentimes the primary reason the potential birthparent is choosing adoption is because they want their child to have *two* loving parents.

Make sure your interests do not paint a picture that suggests your lives are separate. If you talk only about things you like to do separately, then it would be easy to conclude that you do not do anything of interest together.

If your family was really close growing up, make sure to include that. Talk about some of the things your family liked to do for fun when you were growing up.

Even though you already filled out mountains of paperwork about yourself, the profile letter is probably the only thing read by a potential birthparent. Do not expect them to know something about you if it was in your other paperwork but not in your profile letter.

While you are trying hard to make sure this letter does not come off like a resume, you still want to make sure you include some of your successes. If you have a college degree, you definitely want to put that in your letter. Talk a little about what you do for a living and where you plan to go with your career.

It is important to include what your roles are in the home. If you believe in having a mother who does not work outside the home but stays at home with the children, you will want that in there. If you believe the opposite, that women are valuable in the workforce to help make a better living for the family, then that needs to be included. Perhaps the roles in your home are unique to your family. Either way, this detail could be a deal-breaker for some potential birthparents (especially potential birthmothers).

Make sure you include your thoughts on open vs. closed adoption. You owe it to yourself, to your future child, and to the future birthparents to educate yourself on open adoption relationships. There are three other short books in this series that can help you with that.

The best way to learn about open adoption relationships is to learn from experience. Read people's stories. I have written a three book series to tell our story with adoption (our first adoption, our second adoption, and a short follow-up book six years later). You can receive book one of that series by simply emailing me to ask for it at russell.ira.elkins@gmail.com and I will send you book one of the series for **free** (via email in ebook form) entitled *Open Adoption, Open Heart*. By reading other people's stories, you will be able to ask yourself how you feel about certain aspects of open adoption relationships and consider what you would do if you were in someone else's shoes. Open adoption relationships are unusual and unique. You cannot expect to know what you want if you have not given it sufficient thought.

You should never promise in your profile letter— or anywhere else— the kinds of things open adoption would require if you do not know you can fulfill them. It is common for potential birthparents to read letters looking specifically for that information. It is your obligation to learn as much as you can about the process; it is not something to take lightly. If it appears in your letter that you are avoiding the topic or have not given it much thought, many potential birthparents will not consider you to adopt their child.

Do not make the mistake of thinking all potential birthparents want extremely interactive open adoption relationships. Some will want that, others will not. While most adoptions today have at least a small level of interaction between the adoptive family and the biological parents, some birthparents do not want an open adoption at all. So be sure to include at least some information about what level of interaction you are comfortable with.

Keep in mind that birthparents do not ever want to feel like they are a burden on you, so choose wording like, "We are excited to share photographs" rather than "We are willing to share photographs." For some potential birthparents, even though it may not be more than a couple of sentences, knowing whether or not you are interested in having an open adoption can be the most important piece of your letter.

How Should the Letter End?

Similarly to how you began your letter, thank the reader for taking the time to get to know you. Do not say anything presumptuous like, "We look forward to hopefully raising your child." Those types of things make you sound pushy.

Include some of your thoughts about adoption in general. This could include things like how you plan to talk to your children, even from a young age, about their adoptive roots.

Make sure to conclude with some information on how they can contact you. Chances are you already gave all that information to the adoption agency or caseworker, but if your agency allows it, they may prefer to contact you directly. Include your email address if that is how you want to be contacted. Most agencies advise against including your home address or phone number on your profile. You can always provide that later, after being contacted, if that is the type of relationship you want.

Last but not least, put a link to your blog. If you do not have a blog, you are cutting yourself short.

What Are Some Other Things to Keep in Mind with the Letter?

It is a good idea to point out that you are aware they are making difficult decisions, but never say that you know what they are going through unless you are a birthparent who has placed a child for adoption. Their situation is unique in this world. Even if you have lost a child or your ex-wife never lets you see your children, do not say you understand their pain or that you have been in their shoes. Imagining so will probably turn off any interest they may have in you.

Do not beg. Potential birthparents will be interested in people they either look up to or see as peers. Begging inevitably makes you look pathetic. This includes saying things like, "Please do us a favor and take time to look at our blog." You would be better served to say, "Here is a link to our blog if you would like to get to know us better."

Avoid making yourself look like you want their pity. The majority of hopeful adoptive parents have a pity story, whether it is infertility or something else. Potential birthparents are going through what will be one of their toughest trials in life. Feel free to mention your infertility, but stay away from talking about just how difficult your trials are. Spending your time on the depression you have felt with infertility may turn off the reader because they could either feel like you are trying to compare and compete about who has the bigger trial, or they might think they have enough on their own plate and they do not want to take on more trials (yours) along with you.

Do not pretend to enjoy something you do not or be someone you are not. If you manage to fool someone into believing a falsehood, the truth will eventually come out. Just present who you truly are because someone will appreciate you for your uniqueness.

Do not brag about yourself. Sure, you want the potential birthparents to know your best qualities, but nobody likes to listen to someone boast.

I have seen many couples choose to brag about their spouse, though, which is not the same thing. The way to go about doing this is the hopeful adoptive dad would write about what a wonderful person his lovely wife is, and vice versa. In bragging and boasting about one another, you can talk about all the wonderful qualities both of you have without coming across as pompous. In fact, if you do it right, it can come across as endearing to see how much the two hopeful adoptive parents look up to each other.

Do not use a bunch of big words in your letter, even if you are the type of person who likes to use big words in your regular speech. The reason is not because potential birthparents do not understand big words. No, the reason is because people who overuse big words can come across as someone trying too hard to appear smart. People who come across that way tend to be seen as condescending.

Proofread. Proofread. Proofread. And then have a trusted friend proofread for you. Many people are not great spellers, and that is okay. Many people do not have the best grammar, and that is okay too. What is not okay is to assume that you can leave your letter full of misspellings and mistakes and assume it does not matter. While it is true that it will make you look uneducated, something more important than that is that it makes you look like you do not care—like you are not putting much effort into your adoption. I guarantee there is someone close to you who has a decent grasp on the English language who would be willing to help you out. And even if you have a great grasp on grammar and spelling, that does not mean you couldn't use a second brain and second pair of eyes on what you have written. This concept is something that I (like all writers) have had come to terms with. Every book I write gets picked apart by my editors, and when I am humble enough to accept their help, I love the end result. Your friends are cheering for you with this adoption. They will be willing to help you out.

3

YOUR BLOG

Your profile cover photo will be the first level of contact a potential birthparent could have with you. Your goal with that photo is simply to be noticed. Your second level of contact is that of your profile letter and photos where your goal is let them get to know you enough that hopefully they find you interesting. Still, someone who has read your letter and perused your pictures could hardly say they know you.

Your blog is a whole new level in this progression. While your profile letter is well-organized and somewhat formal, your blog is going to be more casual and spontaneous.

Your blog is completely separate from the profile you have listed with the agency. If you do not know anything about starting one, don't worry. Just do a simple Google search about how to create one or find a tutorial on YouTube. The companies who provide this service do all they can to make their blog platforms user-friendly.

If you do not want to pay money for a web page or blog address, there are plenty of places that offer free spaces that will work perfectly well for what you need.

With a blog, you can update your pictures or writings as often as you want without having to go through the agency. With a blog you can write as often and as much as you want without having to delete any of your old posts. You can (and should) include as many pictures as you want. A blog is a great way to help potential birthparents see what you are really like because on your blog you are going to truly be yourself. You are going to let your hair down. You are not going to worry about whether or not you are wearing makeup. You are not even going to be too worried about whether or not your pictures are high quality. Everyone loves to look through pictures, especially when they are trying to understand what life might be like in someone else's world.

With most adoption agencies, it is not practical to update your pictures or profile letter very often. Because of this, the information included in your adoption agency profile listing is about your life generally. It does not include current specifics about your daughter's dance recital last week or how awesome your tomatoes are turning out this summer in your garden. Your blog can have all of those wonderful things included in it. If someone has made it this deep into wanting to get to know you, then you want them to have plenty to feed upon. Give them all kinds of pictures from your day-to-day life—Little League, Christmas parties, repainting the walls inside the house, the stuff that makes you a normal person.

You have already expressed in your profile letter whether or not you want to have an open adoption. If you said you are interested in that type of relationship, this blog can be a comforting indication that you have that ability to be open. It can serve as proof that you are not afraid to share your personal life.

profile pictures from our first and second adoption

Adoption Profile

We can't begin to tell you how much love and respect we have for everybody who makes the difficult decision to place a child for adoption. We have been unable to have our own children, so we're incredibly grateful and excited about the prospect of adoption. Thank you for taking a moment to get to know us a little bit by reading our letter to you.

About Us

Our story began on a Sunday morning in church. With a little over a year left in college, Russell had just moved into a new apartment. Jammie had just moved to town a few days earlier and was staying with her parents while she looked for her own place. The timing couldn't have been any better. If Russell had moved to his new apartment a few weeks later, Jammie would have already been living in her place fifteen miles away. If Jammie had moved to the area a few weeks earlier, Russell wouldn't have spent that first Sunday with his eyes glued to the beautiful blonde across the room. It didn't take Russell very long to have her cornered as he introduced himself and found out her name. All of the usual steps of dating and going home to meet each other's families soon followed, and before long Russell was nervously standing in front of Jammie's father asking for his blessing to marry his daughter.

Jammie was born in Utah. She grew up being the only girl and the youngest sibling in the house until, when Jammie was 11 years old, her younger sister was born. Jammie would spend part of the day roughhousing with her three older brothers and then the rest of the day playing on the floor with her baby sister. She doesn't wrestle with her brothers anymore, and her baby sister is now a teenager, but it is still just as enjoyable to get together as a family.

Russell was born in Maryland and grew up as the fourth child out of six. While the Navy had Russell's family moving around a lot, he spent the majority of his younger years living in Nevada. He loved catching lizards and playing football or baseball with his siblings and friends out in the desert sand. All of Russell's siblings have moved out of Nevada, but everyone is still within driving distance and enjoys getting together as often as possible.

While growing up, Jammie's family watched rodeos and rode horses while Russell's family preferred watching baseball and tossing the ball around. Jammie's dad built saddles and programmed computers, while Russell's dad was a hospital administrator for the Navy. Jammie lived in the same house until she was 17 years old, while Russell lived in 10 different houses before he left for college at age 17. Jammie's house was mostly decorated with a country style, while Russell's house was mostly decorated with paintings and stained glass art done by family members. With all of the differences in styles, though, the similarities are much stronger. Both families love to keep in close contact. Both families love to get together whenever possible to ride horses or play softball. Both families would do anything for each other, and both families love each other more than anything.

How We Live

Russell graduated from college with a bachelor's degree in sociology and also graduated from a technical school with a degree as a dental laboratory technician. He worked for a few years under someone else before he and Jammie started their own dental lab business. At work in the dental lab, Russell does the majority of the work required to make gold and porcelain crowns, veneers, bridges, etc. Jammie assists in the initial phases of the crown-making process by making models of the teeth, and she's also very good at handling the majority of the business's organization and finances, both of which she does from home. Jammie looks forward to being a stay-at-home mother once a little one arrives into the home.

After graduating from college and moving to Boise, we spent the first few months searching for our perfect home. We weren't allowed any pets when we were living in our college apartment, so we were almost as excited to be able to get a dog as we were about getting our own house. On the first day we could move into our new house, we unloaded one truckload of our belongings and then went to pick out a dog, even before we went to get the second truckload of stuff. We now have two dogs, Bogey and Mulligan, and we chose them because their breeds are great as family dogs. Most of our friends have children, and our nieces and nephews are over all the time, so both dogs are great with kids.

Our Interests

We're never short of pictures from any event. Jammie loves photography and takes her nice camera just about everywhere she goes. She mostly photographs weddings or family portraits, but she's done photo shoots with just about anyone or anything, and they all turn out beautifully. The only problem with her photography is that Russell often forgets to take the camera out of her hands, so she's not in as many pictures as he is.

When Russell was a teenager he never skipped a day of practicing his guitar. On most days, he'd come home late from working at the grocery store with his body being tired but his mind telling him otherwise. He would tell himself he'd just play for five minutes or so, but he always ended up strumming his six-string well past bedtime. The many hours of practice paid off. Russell has a band with two of his brothers who play with him on stage all around the Boise area. They are currently working on recording their fifth album.

Russell and Jammie both love to be active with all kinds of sports. Russell played baseball for his high school baseball team, so when he married Jammie, she took up the sport and has played on softball teams with him. Jammie played on her high school basketball team, so when she married Russell, he took up the sport too. Russell discovered disc golf (Frisbee golf) a few years before meeting Jammie, so she took up the sport and both have won many tournaments all around Idaho and Utah. Jammie discovered volleyball a few years before meeting Russell, so he took up that sport as well, and they have fun playing together on city league teams or just with other friends. Whatever sport it is, Russell and Jammie have probably tried it and enjoyed it.

No matter what our interest is, we enjoy doing it together. Jammie often comes up on stage to sing a song or two with Russell while he's performing. Russell goes with Jammie from time to time to help her out with a photo shoot. Simply spending time together is the most important part. Russell and Jammie are best friends.

Thank You

We can't fully understand everything you are going through, but we want you to know that we respect and love you very much. When that happy day does come and we're able to start our family, we look forward to having an open and loving relationship with our children's birthparents. We're excited to share updates as well as pictures, building our open relationship as we go. Again, thank you so much for taking the time to get to know us. If you'd like to see the current updates on our blog, or if you'd like to contact us, you can find us at:

xxxxxxx.blogspot.com

xxxxxxx@gmail.com